GREGORY L. VOGT

URANUS

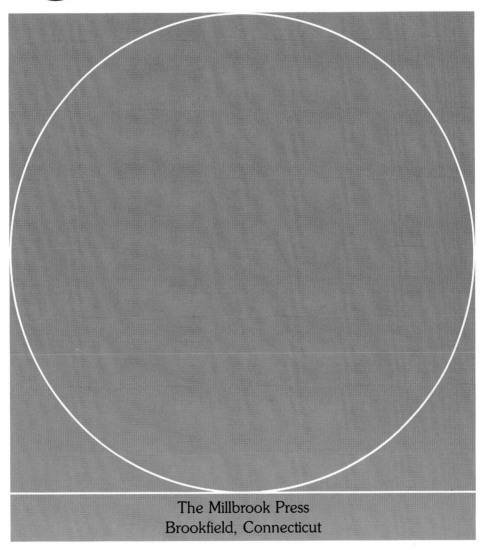

The Millbrook Press
Brookfield, Connecticut

Published by The Millbrook Press
2 Old New Milford Road
Brookfield, Connecticut 06804

Library of Congress Cataloging-in-Publication Data

Vogt, Gregory.
Uranus/Gregory L. Vogt.
p.   cm.—(Gateway solar system)
Includes bibliographical references and index.
Summary: An introduction to the bluish-green planet,
discovered in 1781 by Sir William Herschel.
ISBN 1-56294-330-8 (lib. bdg.)
1. Uranus (Planet)—Juvenile literature.
[1. Uranus (Planet)] I. Title. II. Series:
Vogt, Gregory. Gateway solar system.
QB681.V64   1993
523.4'7—dc20   92-30184   CIP   AC

Photographs and illustrations courtesy
National Aeronautics and Space Administration

Solar system diagram by Anne Canevari Green

URANUS

In the spring of 1977 a jet airplane climbed high over the vast expanse of the Indian Ocean. It was nighttime, and riding inside the plane were *astronomers*—scientists who study objects in outer space. They were chasing a rare event.

The planet Uranus, moving in its *orbit* (path) around the sun, was going to pass in front of a very distant star. The star was so faint that it could be seen only with a telescope. And you had to be in just the right place to see Uranus pass in front of it. The airplane was the Kuiper Airborne Observatory of the National Aeronautics and Space Administration (NASA). It had a window through which a large telescope could peer at the sky above.

The astronomers wanted to see what happened when Uranus passed in front of the star. Just moments before that would happen, the star's light would pass through Uranus's atmosphere. From the way the star's light faded in Uranus's atmosphere, they would be able to tell how thick the atmosphere was and even what its

---

◀ A crescent view of Uranus, photographed by the *Voyager 2* spacecraft.

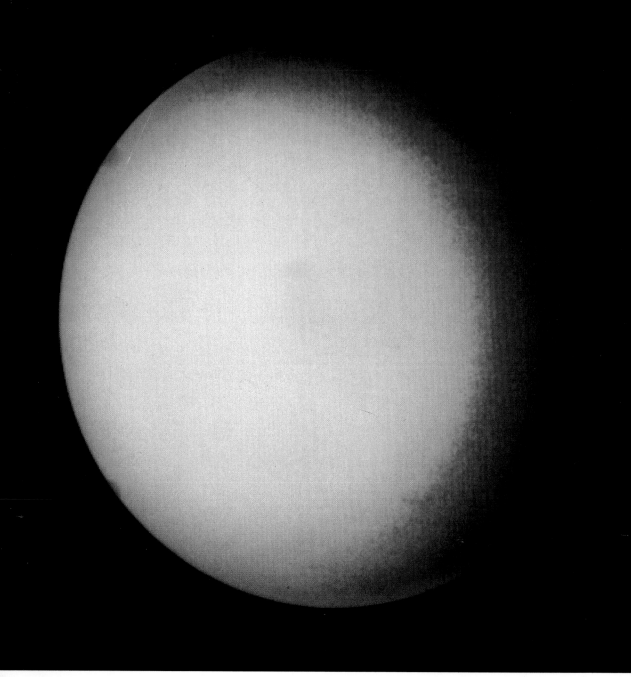

Uranus appears pale and colorless in this *Voyager* picture.

temperature was. They could also make a very precise measurement of Uranus's diameter.

Everything was going very well. Then, about 35 minutes before Uranus was to pass in front of the star, something unexpected happened. The light of the star dimmed for several seconds. A few minutes later it happened again. The light dimmed three more times before Uranus blocked the star's light altogether. Later, when Uranus moved away from the star, the star's light dimmed five more times.

The excited astronomers realized that they had made an important discovery. The star's light was being dimmed because it was passing behind *rings*. The astronomers detected five rings, made of particles of rock and ice, surrounding Uranus.

At the time of the discovery, Uranus was only the second planet known to have a ring system. Saturn was the first. Today, we know that the four giant planets of our solar system—Jupiter, Saturn, Uranus, and Neptune—all have ring systems.

The Seventh Planet

Uranus is the seventh planet of our solar system. It orbits the sun at a distance of 1,785 million miles (2,873 mil-

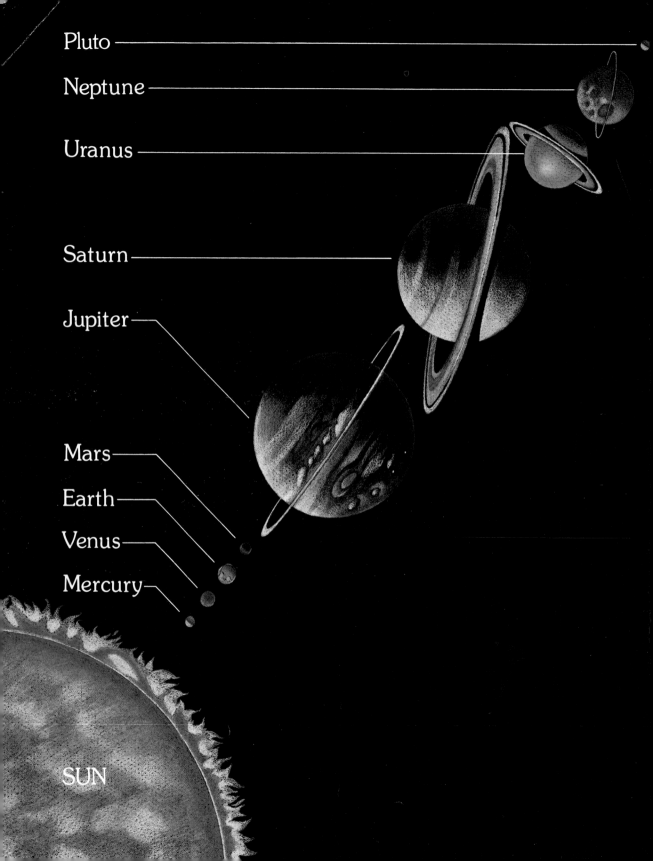

Pluto

Neptune

Uranus

Saturn

Jupiter

Mars

Earth

Venus

Mercury

SUN

lion kilometers). Because it is so far out in deep space, Uranus is very difficult to see. You need a small telescope to see it, and you need to know where to look. For this reason Uranus, unlike many of the other planets, wasn't known by ancient astronomers.

Uranus was discovered in 1781 by an amateur astronomer. Sir William Herschel was a musician who had a great interest in astronomy. He couldn't afford to buy a big telescope, so he made his own. One night in March 1781, Herschel was studying the constellation of Gemini. He spotted a blue-green dot that proved, after several nights of viewing, to be moving very slowly across the sky.

At first, Herschel believed he had discovered a comet. But as word of his discovery spread, professional astronomers measured the distance to the object and decided it was too far away to be a comet. It must be a planet instead. The new planet, twice as far from the sun as Saturn, was eventually named Uranus.

Uranus is huge compared to Earth. Its diameter is 31,764 miles (51,118 kilometers), about four times Earth's diameter. In fact, Uranus is the third largest planet in the solar system, after Jupiter and Saturn.

The atmosphere of Uranus is made up mainly of hydrogen and helium gases, with a small amount of

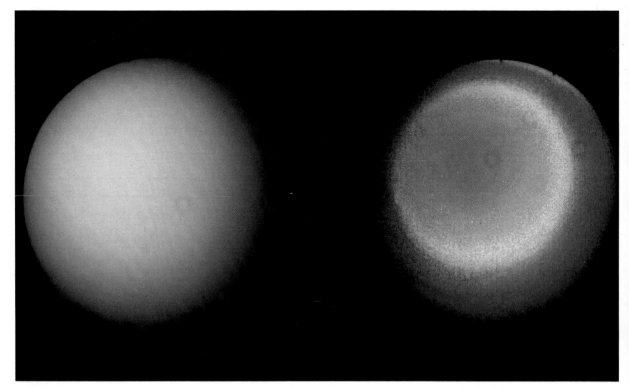

Two views of Uranus show its atmospheric haze. The picture on the right has been changed by a computer to show some of the structure in the atmosphere around the planet's north pole.

methane and other gases. The methane gives Uranus its blue-green color. That's because methane absorbs some of sunlight's colors, leaving bluish-green light to reflect back into space.

The upper atmosphere of Uranus is cloudy and very active, or turbulent. Strong winds blow the blue-green gas around the planet. Near the planet's *equator*, winds have been clocked at speeds of nearly 650 miles (1,040 kilometers) per hour.

Around Uranus's south pole, the atmosphere has an odd appearance. Sunlight seems to be reacting with the chemicals there to create what looks like *smog*. (On Earth, smog is the smoky haze produced when air pollution from automobiles, homes, and industry undergoes chemical reactions in sunlight.)

Scientists are not sure what lies below Uranus's thick, cloudy atmosphere. Some astronomers believe that about 5,000 miles (8,000 kilometers) below the cloud tops is an ocean of water and ammonia. The ocean may be over 6,000 miles (10,000 kilometers) deep. Beneath the ocean is a core of heavier materials. This core is thought to be as large as Earth.

One of the strangest things about Uranus is that the planet is tipped on its side.

Imagine a model of the solar system sitting on top of a large round table. A large ball, placed in the center, represents the sun. All the planets are spinning tops that orbit (travel around) the sun in great circles.

No two planets are tilted in exactly the same direction. But the *axis* of each planet points more or less up-and-down—except for Uranus and the much more distant planet Pluto. (An axis is an imaginary line running through a planet from its north to its south pole.) Uranus is lying on its side—its axis is sideways! (So is Pluto's.) Uranus is spinning too, but it spins on its side.

Because of this tilt, once each Uranus year (about 84 Earth years long) the sun appears almost directly over Uranus's north pole. Half a Uranus year later, the sun is almost directly over the planet's south pole. Some astronomers think the reason that planets tilt in different directions is that they collided with other objects in the early history of the solar system. In the case of Uranus, an object as large as Earth may have collided with the planet, tipping Uranus's axis over.

A Spacecraft Arrives

Although astronomers have been studying Uranus with their telescopes since 1781, we have learned much of what we know about the planet from one event. In January 1986, NASA's *Voyager 2* spacecraft made a visit to Uranus.

Voyager 2 had been on a remarkable space voyage that began in 1977 when it was rocketed from Earth. In

The first close-up view of Uranus was taken by *Voyager 2*. In this picture ▷ *Voyager* is only two and a half hours from its closest approach.

Uranus's rings (left), given pastel colors by a computer to make details easier to see. The smallest details are 25 miles (40 km) across. Two extreme close-ups of one of the rings (right) show many smaller lines within the ring.

1979 the spacecraft visited Jupiter, and in 1981 it flew past Saturn. This was the first time a single spacecraft had flown by three planets. *Voyager 2* carried television cameras, scientific instruments, and a radio to send the data it collected back to Earth.

When *Voyager 2* arrived at Uranus, astronomers already knew that the planet had five moons and nine rings. (Four more rings had been discovered after the first discovery of five.) By the time *Voyager 2* left the planet, astronomers had found another ten moons and two more rings. The spacecraft also measured the length of Uranus's day to be 17 hours, 14 minutes.

Voyager's measurements of Uranus's rings show that they are made up of boulder-size chunks of very dark material. The chunks are so dark that they reflect only a

Uranus's rings are so dark that when they are brightened by a computer, the black sky behind them appears speckled.

tiny amount of the sunlight that falls on them. That is why they are so difficult to see from Earth.

Another thing *Voyager 2* observed about Uranus is that the space around the planet glows. The mysterious glow extends from the planet's cloud tops to a distance of several thousand miles. Scientists have called the light "electroglow."

The Moons of Uranus

Uranus has 15 known moons, or *satellites*. (A satellite is a small body that orbits a larger body in space. Moons are "natural satellites" that orbit planets. Orbiting space-craft are sometimes called "artificial satellites" because they are made by humans.) Ten of those moons were unknown before *Voyager* visited the planet.

The five previously known moons are named for characters in plays by William Shakespeare. They are Oberon, Titania, Umbriel, Ariel, and Miranda. These moons range in size from 293 to 982 miles (472 to 1,580 kilometers) in diameter.

Many *Voyager* pictures of Uranus and several of its moons combined in one picture. Shown is Uranus (blue) and the satellites Ariel, Miranda, Titania, Oberon, and Umbriel. The moons and Uranus are not shown in their correct relative sizes. ▶

The five large moons of Uranus are partly rock and partly ice. They are all cold and dark gray in color. All show signs of past activity, including ice sheets and giant cracks like those caused by earthquakes on Earth.

Titania is Uranus's largest moon, 982 miles (1,580 kilometers) in diameter. This moon has a surface that is cut with huge cracks and canyons. They were probably created by movements of the moon's crust.

Titania has craters from *meteor* collisions in its surface, but none that are very large. Large impact craters are very common throughout the solar system. It is likely that Titania once had large craters but something erased

Titania, Uranus's largest moon, in a *Voyager 2* photo taken about 300,000 miles (about 500,000 km) away. The picture shows many craters and a bright trench-like feature on the left.

them. Perhaps early in Titania's history, heat from its interior melted the icy surface. When Titania cooled, new ice covered the large craters.

Oberon is the second largest of Uranus's moons, 947 miles (1,524 kilometers) in diameter. It is the farthest out of the planet's moons, circling Uranus at a distance of 362,021 miles (582,600 kilometers). Oberon has been peppered with meteors so that its surface looks like Swiss cheese. *Voyager 2*'s close look revealed large cracks cutting across the southern hemisphere of the moon.

Oberon has several large, bright craters that appear

Oberon's face shows craters, including one with a central peak near the center. A mountain peak juts out into space along the lower left side of the moon.

An oval, resembling a doughnut, on the upper right edge of Umbriel. Although they are difficult to see in this picture, meteor craters cover Umbriel's surface.

to be filled with lava flows. Because water is so plentiful on all the Uranian moons, it is likely that Oberon's "lava" is really ice. Water mixed with dark material appears to have flooded onto the moon's surface, filling some of the craters there.

Another moon, Umbriel, has a very dark surface that reflects much less sunlight than do Uranus's other large satellites. That is because this moon seems to have a thin coating of some dark material spread out over its surface. Umbriel also appears to have a thick crust that is not easily marked by small meteorite impacts.

Umbriel is a bit bland when compared to Uranus's other moons. But it has two interesting features. One is a mysterious white oval mark, resembling a doughnut, that scientists haven't explained yet. The other is a light-colored mountain peak in the center of a dark crater. When a large meteor struck Umbriel, the rock melted and splashed up in the middle of the crater that the meteorite formed. Before the melted rock could settle back down, it froze to form the mountain.

The surface of Ariel, Uranus's fourth largest moon, is cut by many cracks that have formed long valleys.

The weirdest of all of Uranus's moons—and one of the strangest moons in the entire solar system—is Miranda. Miranda is about 293 miles (472 kilometers) in diameter and orbits Uranus at a distance of 80,656 miles (129,800 kilometers).

Miranda's surface is like a cracked china cup. It is crossed by huge canyons as deep as 12 miles (20 kilometers). It also has winding valleys and crater-pocked plains. The really strange thing about Miranda is that the moon appears to have been smashed into large pieces in a collision with an *asteroid*. But, instead of breaking

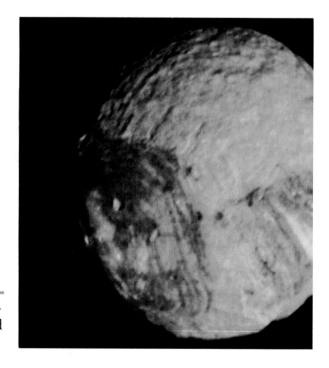

Miranda has many parallel ridges and valleys and bands of colors.

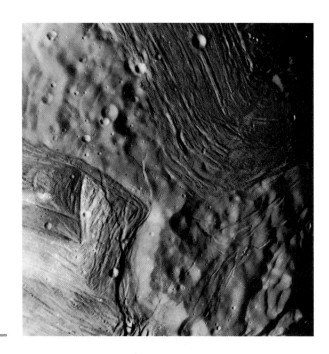

Voyager 2 took this photograph of an unusual V-shaped figure on Miranda's surface.

up to form several new moons, the pieces were somehow "glued" back together. Perhaps Miranda partly or completely melted in the heat of the impact. Then, before the pieces could harden, they fell back together and stuck to each other.

The largest of the newly discovered moons is only 96 miles (154 kilometers) in diameter. Their small size partly explains why these moons were not found until *Voyager 2* arrived. At Uranus's great distance from Earth, they were just too tiny to be seen with telescopes.

Another reason these moons were so hard to see is

that they are all very dark. If you could place a piece of white paper behind each of these moons, they would appear as black as lumps of coal.

Like the known moons, the new moons of Uranus were named after characters in plays by Shakespeare. They have names like Puck, Cordelia, and Juliet. Puck is the largest of the newly discovered moons, and Cordelia is the smallest (16 miles, or 26 kilometers, in diameter). Cordelia is also the closest moon to Uranus. It orbits at a distance of 30,914 miles (49,750 kilometers) from the planet's cloud tops. That places this moon within some of Uranus's rings.

Future Study

Voyager 2 passed by the seventh planet and headed farther out into deep space. The spacecraft took advantage of Uranus's *gravitation* to bend its course and aim itself for another planetary encounter, this time with the planet Neptune.

Unfortunately, *Voyager 2* will be the only spacecraft to visit Uranus for a very long time. No missions to the giant planets beyond the orbit of Saturn are being considered. When a new mission is planned, it may take a

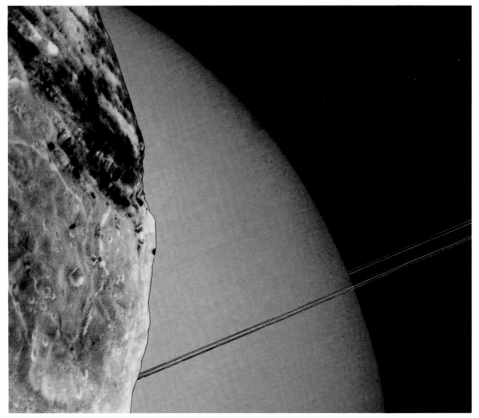

Several *Voyager* images combined to show what Uranus might look like from the surface of Miranda. Cracks and valleys are seen on Miranda's surface.

decade before the spacecraft is ready for launch and perhaps a decade more for it to actually arrive.

Scientists will probably use NASA's Hubble Space Telescope (HST) to study Uranus. But the HST's view won't be as clear as the pictures gathered by *Voyager 2* when it swept to within 51,000 miles (82,000 kilometers) of the planet's cloud tops.

Still, even though astronomers won't have another opportunity to send a spacecraft to Uranus for a very long time, they have a great amount of information from *Voyager 2*'s encounter to study. Astronomers will be busy studying that data for many years, for there is still much to learn about the blue-green planet.

URANUS QUICK FACTS

Uranus: Named for the Greek son and husband of Gaea (Earth) and the father of Saturn and grandfather of Jupiter.

	Uranus	Earth
Average Distance From the Sun		
Millions of miles	1,785	93
Millions of kilometers	2,873	150
Revolution (one orbit around the sun)	84.01 years	1 year
Average Orbital Speed		
Miles per second	4.2	18.6
Kilometers per second	6.8	30
Rotation (spinning once)	17 hours, 14 minutes	24 hours
Diameter at Equator		
Miles	31,764	7,926
Kilometers	51,118	12,756
Surface Gravity (compared to Earth's)	0.9	1
Mass (the amount of matter contained in Uranus, compared to Earth)	14.5	1
Atmosphere	hydrogen helium	nitrogen oxygen
Satellites (moons)	15	1
Rings	11	0

Uranus's Moons	*Diameter*	*Distance From Planet*
Cordelia	16 mi	30,914 mi
	26 km	49,750 km

Uranus's Moons	Diameter	Distance From Planet
Ophelia	20 mi	33,412 mi
	32 km	53,770 km
Bianca	27 mi	36,761 mi
	44 km	59,160 km
Cressida	41 mi	38,383 mi
	66 km	61,770 km
Desdemona	36 mi	38,930 mi
	58 km	62,650 km
Juliet	52 mi	40,160 mi
	84 km	64,630 km
Portia	68 mi	41,074 mi
	110 km	66,100 km
Rosalind	34 mi	43,454 mi
	54 km	69,930 km
Belinda	42 mi	46,759 mi
	68 km	75,250 km
Puck	96 mi	53,439 mi
	154 km	86,000 km
Miranda	293 mi	80,656 mi
	472 km	129,800 km
Ariel	720 mi	118,809 mi
	1,158 km	191,200 km
Umbriel	728 mi	165,289 mi
	1,172 km	266,000 km
Titania	982 mi	270,800 mi
	1,580 km	435,800 km
Oberon	947 mi	362,021 mi
	1,524 km	582,600 km

GLOSSARY

Asteroid	A large space rock, usually a half mile (1 kilometer) or larger in size, that orbits the sun.
Astronomer	A scientist who studies planets, moons, stars, and other objects in outer space.
Axis	An imaginary line running through a planet from its north to its south pole.
Equator	An imaginary line running around the middle of a planet and halfway between the planet's north and south poles.
Gravitation	A force that causes all objects to attract each other.
Mass	The amount of matter contained in an object.
Meteor	A piece of rock or metal that shoots through space.
Orbit	The path a planet takes to travel around the sun, or a moon to travel around a planet.
Revolution	One complete orbit of a planet around the sun, or a moon around a planet.
Rings	Boulder-size chunks of dark material orbiting in circles about Uranus.
Rotation	The spinning of a planet or moon around its axis.
Satellite	A small body in space that orbits around a larger body. A satellite may be "natural," as a moon, or "artificial," as a spacecraft.
Smog	A smoky haze that forms on Earth when air pollutants from automobiles, industry, and homes react with each other in sunlight.
Voyager 2	Spacecraft that visited Jupiter in 1979 and flew by Saturn in 1981 and Uranus in 1986.

FOR FURTHER READING

Asimov, I. *Uranus: The Sideways Planet.* Milwaukee: Gareth Stevens, 1988.

Gallant, R. *The Planets, Exploring the Solar System.* New York: Four Winds Press, 1982.

Simon, S. *Uranus.* New York: William Morrow, 1987.

Vogt, G. *Voyager.* Brookfield, Conn.: The Millbrook Press, 1991.

INDEX

ABOUT THE AUTHOR

Gregory L. Vogt works for NASA's Educational Division
at the Johnson Space Center in Houston, Texas.
He works with astronauts in developing educational
videos for schools.

Mr. Vogt previously served as executive director of the
Discovery World Museum of Science, Economics and
Technology in Milwaukee, Wisconsin, and as an eighth-
grade science teacher. He holds bachelor's and master's
degrees in science from the University of Wisconsin at
Milwaukee, as well as a doctorate in curriculum and
instruction from Oklahoma State University.